This Book Belongs To:

_____

For Samea,
Sid's best friend. –DGD Jr.

Edited by Don Menn
Design by Stefanie Liang
Art for this book was created using Photoshop CS3 with a Wacom Intous 2 Tablet.

Printed in Malaysia
10 9 8 7 6 5 4 3 2

Copyright © 2010 David G. Derrick, Jr.
First hardcover edition published 2010.
Second printing, July 2012.

immedium
inspiring a world of imagination

Immedium, Inc.
P.O. Box 31846
San Francisco, CA 94131
www.immedium.com

Library of Congress Cataloging-in-Publication Data

Derrick, David G., 1978-
  Sid the squid and the search for the perfect job / by David G. Derrick, Jr. -- 1st hardcover ed.
    p. cm.
  Summary: With the help of his friend Alice, Sid the giant squid tries many jobs including firefighter, cook, and window washer, in the search for the perfect one.
  ISBN-13: 978-1-59702-021-3 (hardcover)
  ISBN-10: 1-59702-021-4 (hardcover)
  [1. Occupations--Fiction. 2. Individuality--Fiction. 3. Giant squids--Fiction. 4. Squids--Fiction.
5. Marine animals--Fiction.] I. Title.
  PZ7.D4465Si 2010
  [E]--dc22

                            2009028548

Sid
the Squid
and the Search for the Perfect Job

By David G. Derrick, Jr.

immedium • San Francisco, CA

In this wide and wonderful world
there is a job for everyone.
Or at least that's what Sid believed.
Sid was a giant squid who lived in
the dark depths of the ocean.
He had ten useful arms,
more than a turtle, a sea spider,
or even his cousin the octopus.
Sid wanted to find the perfect
job, but didn't know
where to look.

Sid heard from a shoal of fish that the big city was the best place for someone to find a job.

So Sid decided to see for himself.

Sid was a squid out of water and didn't know the first thing about finding a job in the big city. Luckily he met a girl named Alice.

Alice lived in the city and volunteered to help him, "I know lots of people with different jobs that could use someone handy like you."

First Alice took Sid to meet Officer Mitchell. Impressed by all of Sid's arms the policewoman said,

"Why don't you try directing traffic? It seems like the perfect job for someone like you."

Quickly Sid got the hang of guiding cars, trucks, buses, and people across a busy intersection. For a while it seemed like Officer Mitchell was right; directing traffic was perfect for Sid.

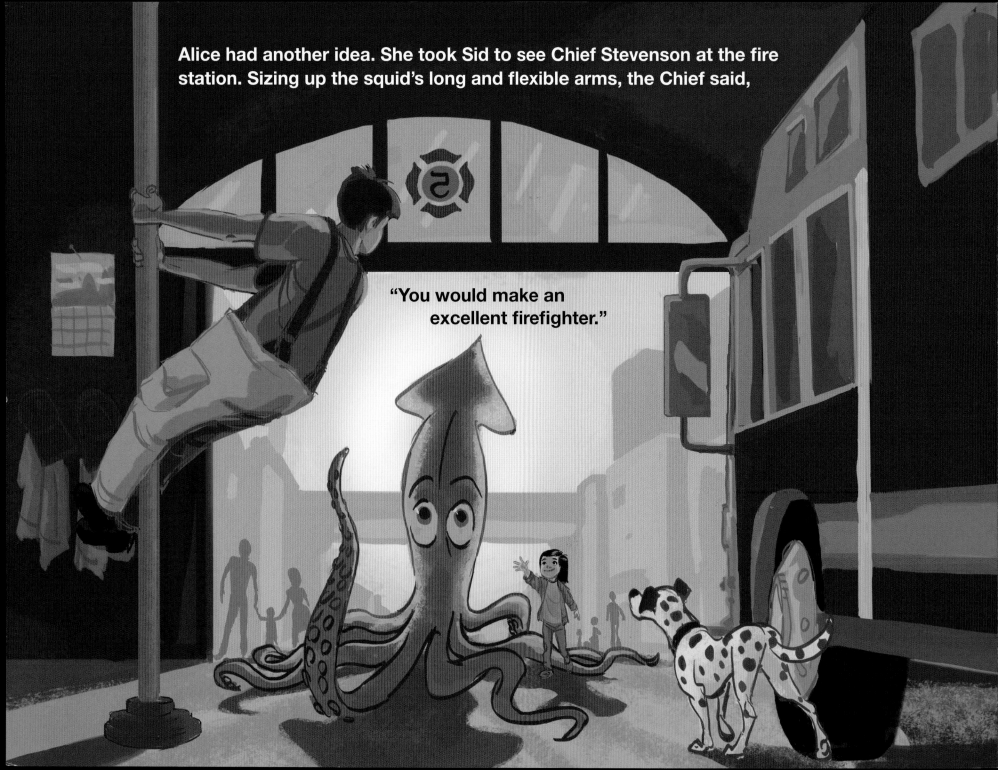

Alice had another idea. She took Sid to see Chief Stevenson at the fire station. Sizing up the squid's long and flexible arms, the Chief said,

"You would make an excellent firefighter."

So Sid became the town's first fire-squid.

Alice and the firemen thought this was a fantastic job for Sid. But he wasn't so sure. Squids need to have wet skin to be happy. Fighting fires was too hot and dry. So Sid and Alice kept looking.

While Sid cooled off in the calm waters by the wharf, Alice saw a restaurant and said, "Aha! Sid, you could be a terrific cook."

Chef Umberto agreed. Sid was amazing!
He could dice carrots, simmer a white sauce, sauté
onions, bake lasagna, and even cook pizzas all at once!
Even Sid thought cooking in the kitchen was the job for him.

That is until someone ordered seafood.

Sid and Alice left the restaurant...but not before releasing all of his new friends into the water.

Finding the perfect job can be tough,
so Alice took Sid to the library.
There Miss Beckstrand, the librarian,
helped them. Searching in books,
magazines, newspapers, and online,
Sid and Alice found lots of new
careers he could try.

Sid auditioned as an actor. He was in luck!
The director wanted to cast Sid in his big movie.
But when Sid read the script, he had second
thoughts about the role. Sid did not want to
act like a monster.

Stage 3

Calamonstro

HE'S HUNGRY

Next Sid climbed tall buildings to wash windows. Unfortunately, his suction cups made them even dirtier.

Sid walked dogs.

Walking dogs was definitely "knot" the right job.

Sid was a one-squid pit crew...

Ouch!

No matter how hard they tried, they couldn't find Sid the right job. He thought that perhaps it was time to quit the big city and go back home.

Splash!

Sid and Alice jumped up when they heard the noise. In the distance, they saw an enormous whale struggling in a net. He needed help!

Instantly Sid swam like
a torpedo out to sea.

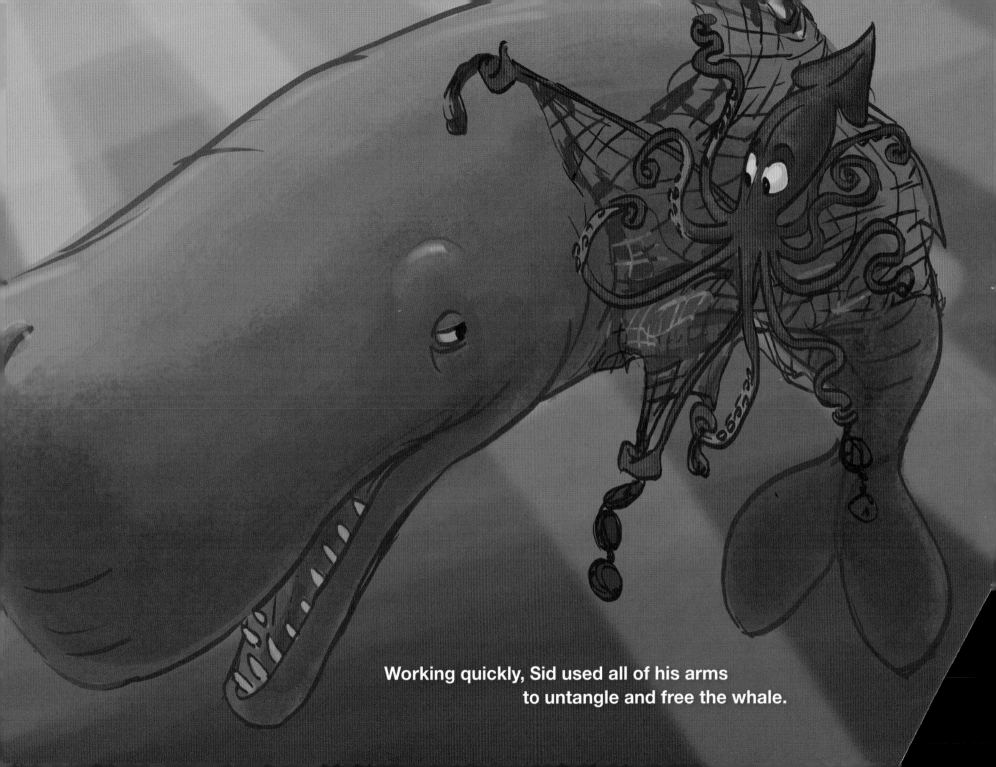

Working quickly, Sid used all of his arms
to untangle and free the whale.

The whale thanked Sid by leaping out of the water.
"Sid you were wonderful!" Alice shouted from
a nearby boat. "These people are animal rescuers
who work at the Aquarium." Sid had never
heard of such a place before.

So Alice took him there. "Sid," continued Alice with a big smile, "I think I've found the perfect job for you."

And she did.
The Aquarium was a wonderful place for someone with ten arms.

He could help his aquatic friends
great and small and...

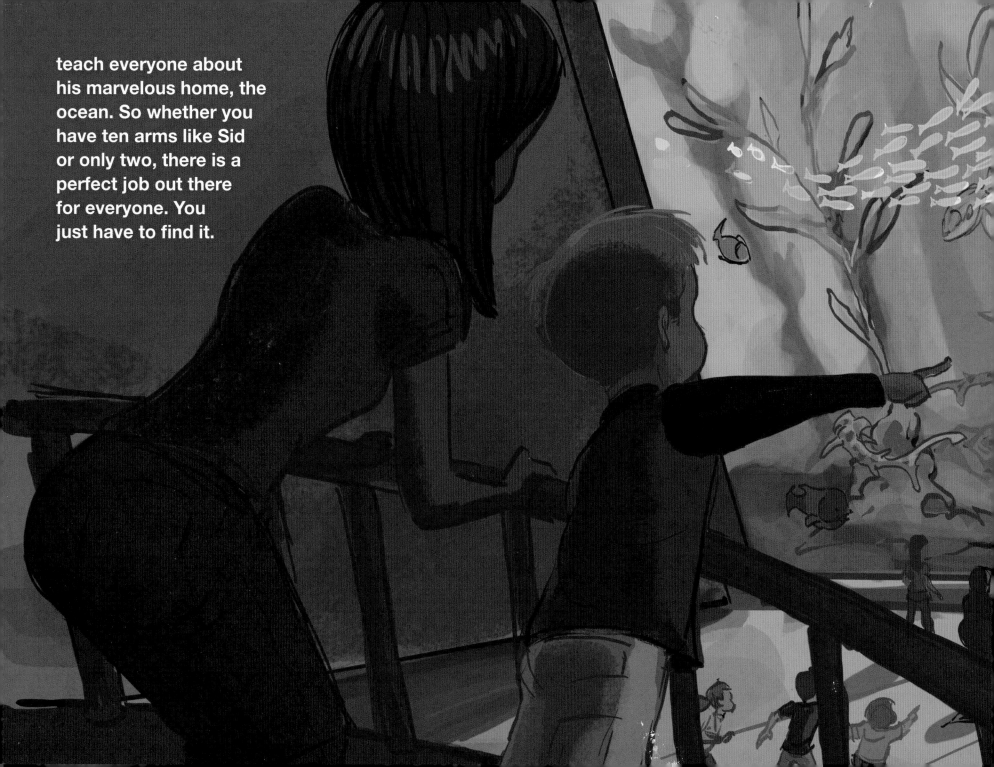

teach everyone about his marvelous home, the ocean. So whether you have ten arms like Sid or only two, there is a perfect job out there for everyone. You just have to find it.